CHEMISTRY EXPLAINED

ELEMENTS & COMPOUNDS

by
Janet Bingham

Minneapolis, Minnesota

Credits

Cover, © ImageFlow/Adobe Stock Images; 4T, © ESA/Johns Hopkins University/NASA; 4B, © VI Studio/Adobe Stock Images; 4–5, © irissca/Adobe Stock Images, 5, © bnenin/Adobe Stock Images; 6T, © anchalee thaweeboon/Shutterstock; 6B, © Atlantist Studio/Shutterstock; 6–7, © Bedrin/Shutterstock; 7T, © zizou7/Shutterstock; 7B, © MRC Laboratory of Molecular Biology/Wikimedia Commons; 8T, © Charles Shapiro/Shutterstock; 8M, © Idutko/Shutterstock; 8B, © MRC Laboratory of Molecular Biology/Wikimedia Commons; 8–9, © Rings and jewelery/Alamy Stock Photo; 10–11, © 2DAssets/Shutterstock and © Art Stocker/Shutterstock; 11T, © Science History Institute/Wikimedia Commons; 11B, © ElenaTlt/Shutterstock; 12T, © 2DAssets/Shutterstock and © trgrowth/Shutterstock; 12B, © Science Source/Science Photo Library; 12–13, © Martyn F. Chillmaid/Science Photo Library; 13, © Turtle Rock Scientific/Science Photo Library; 14T, © Douglas Cliff/Shutterstock; 14B, © Evgeniyqw/Shutterstock; 14–15, © Michael Penev/US Department Of Energy/Science Photo Library; 15, © Welcome Collection; 16T, © Nataliia Budianska/Shutterstock; 16M, © 2DAssets/Shutterstock and © trgrowth/Shutterstock; 16B, © Historic Images/Alamy Stock Photo; 16–17, © RooM the Agency/Alamy Stock Photo; 17T, © YARUNIV Studio/Shutterstock; 18T, © Alexandre Dotta/Science Source/Science Photo Library; 18B, © Bearport Publishing; 18–19, © Max Topchii/Shutterstock; 19T, © New Africa/Shutterstock; 19B, © Kitch Bain/Shutterstock; 20T, © Tawansak/Shutterstock; 20B, © Roman Zaiets/Shutterstock; 20–21, © Ivan Kurmyshov/Shutterstock; 21T, © Feng Yu/Shutterstock; 21B, © Science History Institute/Wikimedia Commons; 22T, © Jo Sam Re/Shutterstock; 22–23, © Tina Gutierrez/Shutterstock; 23T, © Welcome Collection; 24T, © Sergey Merkulov/Shutterstock; 24B, © Ake13bk/Shutterstock; 24–25, © Pozdeyev Vitaly/Shutterstock; 25, © Science History Institute/Wikimedia Commons; 26T, © Kedar Vision/Shutterstock; 26M, © peterschreiber.media/Shutterstock; 26B, © Sansanorth/Shutterstock; 26–27, © Idutko/Shutterstock; 27T, © MarcelClemens/Shutterstock; 27B, © MRC Laboratory of Molecular Biology/Wikimedia Commons; 28T, © LoopAll/Shutterstock; 28–29, © imageBROKER/Alamy Stock Photo; 29, © Harvard University/Wikimedia Commons; 30T, © Adisak Riwkratok/Shutterstock; 30B, © University of Illinois Archives; 30–31, © SritanaN/Shutterstock; 31, © Ali DM/Shutterstock; 32T, © Robert Brook/Science Photo Library/Alamy Stock Photo; 32B, © Lookiepix/Shutterstock; 32–33, © New Africa/Shutterstock; 33, © Tom Hollyman/Science Photo Library; 34T, © Jo Sam Re/Shutterstock; 34B, © Jo Sam Re/Shutterstock; 34–35, © Image Source/Getty Images; 35T, © IT Tech Science/Shutterstock; 35B, © Welcome Collection; 36T, © Sergey Merkulov/Shutterstock; 36B, © Harvard University/Wikimedia Commons; 36–37, © Robert Kneschke/Shutterstock; 37, © ggw/Shutterstock; 38T, © Egoreichenkov Evgenii/Shutterstock; 38B, © buteo/Shutterstock; 38–39, © Sakkmesterke/Science Photo Library; 39T, © OSweetNature/Shutterstock; 39B, © Science History Institute/Wikimedia Commons; 40T, © nguyen thi phuong dieu/Shutterstock; 40BL, © Stephen Mcsweeny/Shutterstock; 40BR, © Maria Symchych/Shutterstock; 40–41, © Halfpoint/Shutterstock; 41, © Bearport Publishing; 42T, © Maruzhenko Yaroslav/Adobe Stock Images; 42B, © D-VISIONS/Shutterstock; 42–43, © Maha Heang/Adobe Stock Image; 43, © andrew_shots/Adobe Stock Images; 44, © Rings and jewelery/Alamy Stock Photo; 45T, © Tawansak/Shutterstock; 45B, © Bedrin/Shutterstock; 47, © Atlantist Studio/Shutterstock

Bearport Publishing Company Product Development Team

Publisher: Jen Jenson; Director of Product Development: Spencer Brinker; Editorial Director: Allison Juda; Editor: Cole Nelson; Editor: Tiana Tran; Production Editor: Naomi Reich; Art Director: Kim Jones; Designer: Kayla Eggert; Designer: Steve Scheluchin; Production Specialist: Owen Hamlin

Statement on Usage of Generative Artificial Intelligence

Bearport Publishing remains committed to publishing high-quality nonfiction books. Therefore, we restrict the use of generative AI to ensure accuracy of all text and visual components pertaining to a book's subject. See BearportPublishing.com for details.

Library of Congress Cataloging-in-Publication Data is available at www.loc.gov or upon request from the publisher.

ISBN: 979-8-89577-498-4 (hardcover)
ISBN: 979-8-89577-540-0 (paperback)
ISBN: 979-8-89577-506-6 (ebook)

© 2026 Arcturus Holdings Limited. This edition is published by arrangement with Arcturus Publishing Limited.

North American adaptations © 2026 Bearport Publishing Company. All rights reserved. No part of this publication may be reproduced in whole or in part, stored in any retrieval system, or transmitted in any form or by any means, electronic, mechanical, photocopying, recording, or otherwise, without written permission from the publisher. Bearport Publishing is a division of FlutterBee Education Group.

For more information, write to Bearport Publishing, 3500 American Blvd W, Suite 150, Bloomington, MN 55431.

Contents

Organizing the Universe 4
Atomic Structure 6
Elements 8
The Periodic Table 10
Element Groups 12
Tiny Hydrogen 14
Alkaline Earth Metals 16
The Halogens 18
Noble Gases 20
Metals 22
Nonmetals and Semimetals 24
Molecules 26
Compounds 28
Organic and Inorganic Chemicals 30
Covalent Bonds 32
Ionic Bonds 34
Reactions 36
Radioactivity 38
Important Properties 40
Elements and Compounds in Our Lives . . . 42

Review and Reflect 44
Glossary 46
Read More 47
Learn More Online 47
Index 48

Organizing the Universe

Everything in our world, including our own bodies, is made of elements. Each element is a type of atom with different properties that make it unique. Over time, scientists have organized these basic building blocks of the universe based on those properties. Most elements are found in nature, but some are synthetic, or made by humans. When two or more elements are combined, they form compounds.

The Elements throughout Time

The leading theory about the origin of the universe is called the big bang theory. It describes how the universe expanded rapidly from an initial state of extreme heat and density around 13.8 billion years ago. Many elements were created shortly after the big bang, including hydrogen and helium. Heavier elements, such as gold and silver, were created later by supernovas.

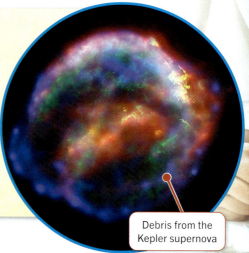

Debris from the Kepler supernova

Household Compounds

Chemists combine elements in labs to synthesize, or create, new compounds with many uses. For example, Teflon is a compound of the elements carbon and fluorine. It is used to coat frying pans, making them nonstick. Nylon is a compound used to make many types of clothing. It combines carbon, oxygen, and hydrogen.

Many gemstones used in jewelry are compounds of several elements that combine to create a range of colors. Rings and bracelets are often made from compounds of metals called alloys.

Changing Shape

When elements combine in a compound, their properties can change drastically. Elements that usually take the form of gases can combine to create solids. Solids can dissolve into liquids, mixing so completely they seem to disappear.

Atomic Structure

All atoms contain even smaller subatomic particles called protons, neutrons, and electrons. The number of these subatomic particles determines the properties of the atom. The variety of atomic structure gives us the 118 elements we know today.

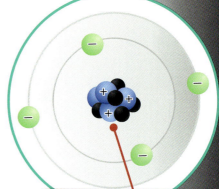

The Atomic Nucleus

The nucleus in the middle of an atom is made up of protons and neutrons. These subatomic particles are packed into a cluster that is 2,000 times heavier than the electrons surrounding the nucleus. An element's atoms all have the same number of protons. This is its atomic number.

Beryllium has an atomic number of 4. Its nucleus has four protons and five neutrons. Four electrons are arranged in two surrounding energy shells.

Electrons

Outside of the nucleus, an atom is mostly empty space. Electrons—subatomic particles with a negative charge—whiz around in energy shells surrounding the nucleus. Each shell is a layer that can hold a set number of electrons, so atoms with more electrons have more shells. The equal and opposite charges of the protons and electrons in an atom attract each other, creating an electromagnetic force that holds the atoms together. On the whole, atoms have the same number of electrons as protons, so the particle has no charge.

Energy shells are stacked inside one another like Russian nesting dolls. But the shells are not solid—only electromagnetic attraction holds the electrons close to the nucleus.

DID YOU KNOW? Protons and neutrons contain even tinier particles called quarks and gluons. Scientists have discovered 36 subatomic particles so far!

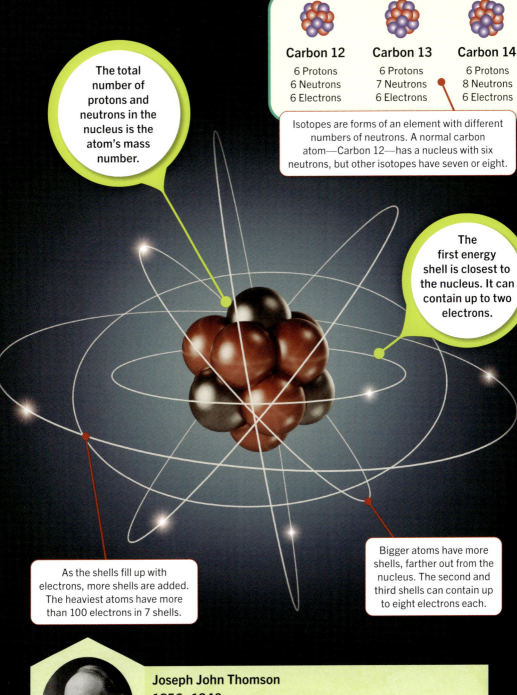

Carbon 12	Carbon 13	Carbon 14
6 Protons	6 Protons	6 Protons
6 Neutrons	7 Neutrons	8 Neutrons
6 Electrons	6 Electrons	6 Electrons

Isotopes are forms of an element with different numbers of neutrons. A normal carbon atom—Carbon 12—has a nucleus with six neutrons, but other isotopes have seven or eight.

The total number of protons and neutrons in the nucleus is the atom's mass number.

The first energy shell is closest to the nucleus. It can contain up to two electrons.

As the shells fill up with electrons, more shells are added. The heaviest atoms have more than 100 electrons in 7 shells.

Bigger atoms have more shells, farther out from the nucleus. The second and third shells can contain up to eight electrons each.

HALL OF FAME

Joseph John Thomson
1856–1940

English physicist J. J. Thomson discovered the electron in 1897. His experiments showed that cathode rays, or the rays seen when electricity flows through gases at low pressure, were streams of particles with much less mass than atoms themselves. We now call these particles electrons. He was awarded the Nobel Prize in Physics in 1906.

Elements

The atoms of different elements have different numbers of protons, neutrons, and electrons. The properties of an element, or the way it looks and behaves, are due to the number of each subatomic particle in its atoms.

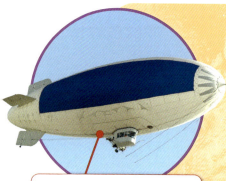

Air is a mixture of gases, including the elements nitrogen, oxygen, and argon. The element in a blimp, helium, is a gas that is lighter than air, so it floats in the sky.

Names and Numbers

We know of 118 elements. Around 90 are found naturally, while the rest are synthetic. Synthetic elements usually have many protons, making them unstable and causing them to decay quickly into elements with fewer protons. Each element is identified by its atomic number, or the number of protons inside one atom's nucleus. And every element is also given a name and a symbol of one or two letters. For example, hydrogen has the symbol H, and lead has the symbol Pb.

All Our Resources

At room temperature, only two elements are liquids—mercury and bromine. Eleven are gases. The rest are solids, with most of these being metals. Some, such as gold, occur naturally in a pure form. However, most elements are found in impure forms as compounds. Elements and their compounds make up the minerals and rocks of Earth's crust.

Silicon oxide, a compound of oxygen and silicon, makes up most of Earth's crust as rocks or sand. Aluminum, iron, and calcium are the next three most common elements in the crust.

HALL OF FAME

Ida Noddack, née Tacke
1896–1978

The element rhenium was first isolated in 1925 in Germany by Ida Tacke, Otto Berg, and Walter Noddack—Ida's future husband. This element has a very high melting point and is now used in aircraft engines. Ida was also the first to suggest that atoms bombarded by neutrons might split into smaller atoms through nuclear fission. Four years later, this was shown to be possible.

Copper is a trace element, meaning there is a tiny amount in your body that keeps you healthy.

We often see gold, silver, and copper made into decorative items, but these metallic elements have many more uses.

Silver is an excellent conductor of heat and electricity. It reflects light effectively as well and is used in mirrors and solar panels.

Gold is very unreactive. It does not react with air and so does not tarnish, or lose its shine. It also conducts electricity well. Because of this, it is used in many electronic devices.

DID YOU KNOW? The most recently discovered element, tennessine, was made in a laboratory in 2010.

9

The Periodic Table

The periodic table neatly displays all the elements by the size of their atoms, which is determined by the number of protons in the nucleus. Each atom has the same number of protons and electrons in its basic form. But every element also has isotopes, or different forms with different numbers of neutrons in the nucleus.

Periods and Groups

Elements on the periodic table are separated into periods, represented by rows, and groups, divided in columns. Groups are elements with similar properties. These groups include metals, nonmetals, halogens, lanthanides and actinides, and noble gases.

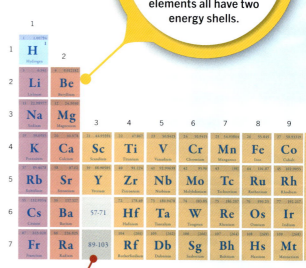

All the elements in a period have the same number of energy shells, in which a certain number of electrons can orbit the nucleus. Period 2 elements all have two energy shells.

The lanthanides and actinides are very similar elements, and so are squeezed in between groups 2 and 3 on the periodic table.

KEY
- Alkali metals
- Alkaline earth metals
- Transition metals
- Other metals
- Other nonmetals
- Halogens
- Noble gases
- Lanthanides
- Actinides

HALL OF FAME

Julia Lermontova
1846–1919

Julia Lermontova had to study in Germany because Russian universities wouldn't take women at the time when she lived. She was only the second woman ever to receive a doctorate in chemistry. Her work on platinum and related metals was respected, and she helped Dmitri Mendeleev fill in the gaps when he organized the elements into the first version of the periodic table.

> All the elements in each group have the same number of electrons in their outer energy shells. This makes them look and behave in similar ways. Group 17 elements all have seven electrons in their outer shell.

What It Tells Us

Each square on the periodic table shows the name, symbol, and atomic number of the element. It also shows the relative weight of the atom—its atomic mass—which relates to the mass of its protons plus neutrons. Atomic mass has a decimal point because it's an average of different isotopes with different neutron counts. Some versions of the periodic table give the mass number, or the total number of protons and neutrons, which is always a whole number.

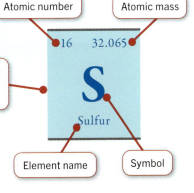

Sulfur (S) has 16 protons in one atom. Its atomic mass number is 32, which means that it has 16 neutrons (32 minus 16).

DID YOU KNOW? People in the Middle Ages swallowed antimony (element 51) to treat constipation. Scientists now know that antimony is toxic.

11

Element Groups

Atoms have energy shells that can hold up to a certain number of electrons. The first, innermost shell can hold two electrons. The second shell holds up to eight electrons. Each shell farther out from the nucleus can hold more electrons. Shells are most stable when they are full, holding their maximum numbers of electrons. Stable elements are less reactive, meaning they do not interact with other atoms as much as unstable elements.

The Outer Shell Electrons

In each group on the periodic table, the elements behave in similar ways because of their pattern of electrons. For example, each group 1 element has one more energy shell than the one before it. So, lithium has two energy shells, sodium has three, and francium has seven. But each element in group 1 has an outermost shell with just one solitary electron. This makes them very reactive, since they are all ready to give up the solitary electron. Elements in other groups are also similar to each other because they have the same number of electrons in their outer shells.

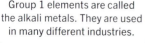

Group 1 elements are called the alkali metals. They are used in many different industries.

HALL OF FAME

Marguerite Catherine Perey
1909–1975

In 1939, francium became the last naturally occurring element to be discovered. It was the only element to be discovered solely by a woman. Marguerite Catherine Perey was separating radioactive elements when she found one that fit a gap in Mendeleev's periodic table, at number 87. She named it francium after her home country, France.

Alkali Metals

The alkali metals are the group 1 elements lithium, sodium, potassium, rubidium, and cesium, plus radioactive francium. These shiny metals are soft enough to cut with a knife. They all react readily with other chemicals, but the ones lower down the table are more reactive than those above. The alkali metals also all react with cold water by releasing heat in an exothermic reaction. Sometimes, they react with nonmetals to form white crystalline salts that dissolve easily in liquids. For example, sodium reacts with chlorine to form sodium chloride, also known as table salt.

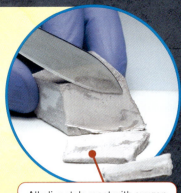

Alkali metals react with oxygen in the air to make metal oxides. The bright, newly cut surface of sodium tarnishes in moments. Potassium reacts even faster!

All alkali metals react with water by giving off hydrogen gas and heat.

Violent reactivity makes the alkali metals very dangerous. Rubidium and cesium explode in water.

Potassium has a spectacular reaction with water. The hydrogen gas it produces bursts into flame. The remaining potassium sparks, catches fire, and may make a small explosion.

Lithium and sodium react less violently with water than potassium. They whiz around on the surface, fizzing with hydrogen gas bubbles, until all the metal is used up.

DID YOU KNOW? Cesium atomic clocks are the most accurate clocks in the world, losing or gaining just one second every 1,400,000 years!

Tiny Hydrogen

The tiny atoms of hydrogen and helium were the first to form just after the creation of the universe. Hydrogen is the smallest atom, with one proton, one electron, and no neutrons. Hydrogen is often shown at the top of group 1, but it's nothing like the solid, soft, shiny alkali metals of group 1. Hydrogen is unique.

Highly Reactive

Pure hydrogen is rare on Earth. It is very reactive, so it's usually found in compounds with other elements. As a nontoxic gas, it is not poisonous. It has no color, smell, or taste. It's also the lightest element, so it is often used in weather balloons high in the atmosphere. It readily explodes with oxygen and burns in air to produce water and energy. Hydrogen is so reactive because it easily shares or gives up its solitary electron.

Hydrogen gas must be kept under pressure to store and move. The element becomes liquid when it's supercooled to −423 degrees Fahrenheit (−253°C).

An early shuttle flight to the International Space Station used about 600,000 gallons (2,250,000 L) of liquid hydrogen as fuel.

Powerful Hydrogen

We wouldn't be here without hydrogen. Life-giving water is made from hydrogen and oxygen atoms. With carbon and other atoms, hydrogen forms the organic chemicals that make up every living thing. Hydrogen gives us fuel via the hydrocarbon molecules of crude oil and natural gas. Pure hydrogen is also becoming more important as a renewable, clean fuel in vehicles. It has been used as rocket fuel since the beginning of space exploration in the 1950s.

DID YOU KNOW? Hydrogen is the most abundant element in the universe. Its atoms make up more than 70 percent of the total mass of all matter.

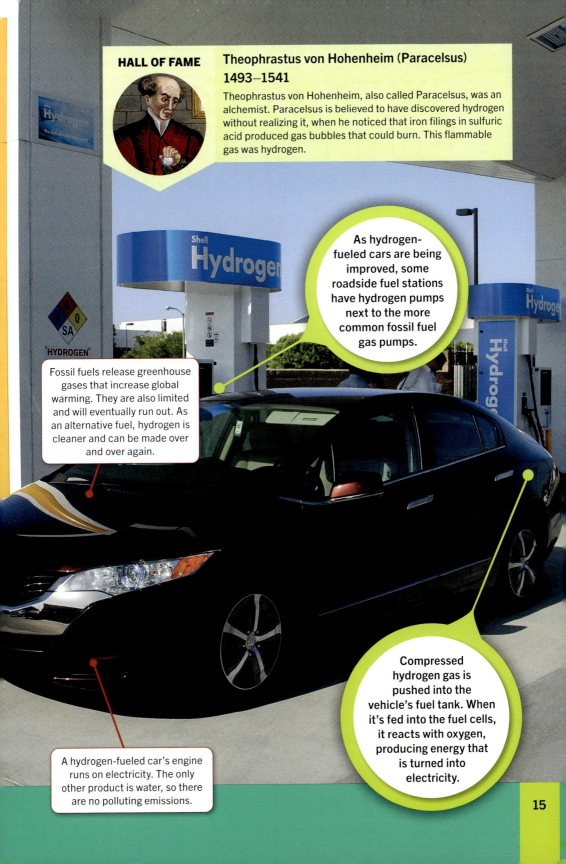

HALL OF FAME

Theophrastus von Hohenheim (Paracelsus) 1493–1541

Theophrastus von Hohenheim, also called Paracelsus, was an alchemist. Paracelsus is believed to have discovered hydrogen without realizing it, when he noticed that iron filings in sulfuric acid produced gas bubbles that could burn. This flammable gas was hydrogen.

As hydrogen-fueled cars are being improved, some roadside fuel stations have hydrogen pumps next to the more common fossil fuel gas pumps.

Fossil fuels release greenhouse gases that increase global warming. They are also limited and will eventually run out. As an alternative fuel, hydrogen is cleaner and can be made over and over again.

Compressed hydrogen gas is pushed into the vehicle's fuel tank. When it's fed into the fuel cells, it reacts with oxygen, producing energy that is turned into electricity.

A hydrogen-fueled car's engine runs on electricity. The only other product is water, so there are no polluting emissions.

15

Alkaline Earth Metals

Group 2 of the periodic table includes the alkaline earth metals beryllium, magnesium, calcium, strontium, barium, and radium. Atoms in this group have two electrons in their outer energy shell. This makes them very reactive, but they are not as reactive as the alkali metals in group 1.

Increasing Reactivity

Like the alkali metals, the alkaline earth metals are silvery or gray, and their reactivity increases as you go down the group. Beryllium, at the top, is the least reactive. It needs a very high temperature before it can react with water. Magnesium, the next element down the group, fizzes a little in cold water, while the reaction is more and more vigorous for calcium, strontium, and barium.

Alkaline earth metals are so reactive that they can exist naturally only as compounds with other elements. The gemstone emerald is a compound of beryllium. Small amounts of chromium make it green.

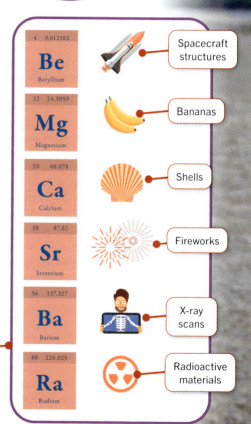

- Be Beryllium — Spacecraft structures
- Mg Magnesium — Bananas
- Ca Calcium — Shells
- Sr Strontium — Fireworks
- Ba Barium — X-ray scans
- Ra Radium — Radioactive materials

Beryllium and magnesium are mixed into lightweight alloys with other metals and used in aircraft and cars. Barium, which is much heavier, helps doctors see inside patients' bodies with X-rays.

HALL OF FAME

Isabella Cortese
Sixteenth Century

Isabella Cortese was a well-traveled Italian alchemist who wrote the first book of cosmetic recipes, which was published in 1561. The book gave advice on running a household and how to make medicines and cosmetics, as well as discussing how metals might be turned into gold. It was very popular and was republished several times.

Alkaline Medicines

The alkaline earth metals get their name because their compounds make solutions with water that are alkaline, the opposite of acidic. Milk of magnesia is a suspension of magnesium hydroxide (H_2MgO_2). It's used as an alkaline medicine to treat indigestion because it neutralizes, or cancels out, the stomach acids that cause the pain.

Magnesium helps the enzymes in our bodies work, so it's important to eat plenty of magnesium-rich foods, such as bananas, nuts, and legumes.

Marine snails make seashells from calcium carbonate. Other invertebrates, such as corals and crabs, also build protective skeletons from calcium compounds.

Pollutants such as sulfur dioxide make acid rain. This softens the skeletons and shells of sea creatures and is harmful to life both in the oceans and on land.

Calcium is essential for all living things. Vertebrates, like us, use calcium compounds to build strong bones and teeth. The main compound in bones is calcium phosphate.

DID YOU KNOW? Up until the 1960s, the hands of some clocks were painted with glow-in-the-dark paints containing radioactive radium!

17

The Halogens

That familiar swimming-pool smell is from compounds of chlorine, the main chemical used to kill germs and keep pools clean. Chlorine is one of the halogens—nonmetal elements in group 17 of the periodic table. Each of the halogens is commonly used in disinfectants. This group includes fluorine, chlorine, bromine, and iodine.

The chlorine in pool sanitizers breaks apart water molecules to create hypochlorous acid (HOCl) and hypochlorite ions (ClO$^-$).

Reactive Group 17

Halogen atoms need only one more electron to reach the maximum, stable number in their outer energy shells. This makes them very reactive. They will readily take an electron from another atom, and so become ions, or particles with a charge. Elements at the top of the group are more reactive. Fluorine's smaller size means the nucleus pulls more strongly on the electrons of other atoms, making it the most reactive of the group.

When heated, iodine changes from a solid to a purple gas without becoming a liquid in between. This is called sublimation.

HALL OF FAME

Henry Aaron Hill
1915–1979

Henry Aaron Hill completed his PhD at Massachusetts Institute of Technology (MIT) and later became the first Black president of the American Chemical Society. He studied compounds used to make fluorine-containing plastics. Hill established companies supplying chemicals used in plastics production, and he offered research and consultation in polymer chemistry.

DID YOU KNOW? Your body contains about 0.0001 ounces (3 mg) of a fluorine compound called fluoride. Fluoride guards against tooth decay.

Ribbon seaweeds take in iodine compounds from seawater, so they are a nutritious food source. Too little iodine in a diet can cause a condition called goiter.

Hypochlorous acid and hypochlorite kill the bacteria and other microorganisms that cause stomach and ear infections.

Chlorine compounds can irritate skin, and hypochlorite makes fabrics fade. So, it's a good idea to rinse your body and your swimsuit when you leave the pool!

Poisons with Useful Compounds

The halogens are strong-smelling, poisonous elements. Their atoms can bond in pairs to form molecules with two identical atoms, but they do not exist in these pure forms in nature. They combine with other elements as compounds in rocks and in the ocean. They react with metals to form ionic salts called metal halides. The halogens behave alike, but they do not all look alike. Fluorine and chlorine are greenish gases, bromine is a red oily liquid, and iodine is a black solid.

Non-stick pans are coated with PTFE (polytetrafluoroethylene), a plastic made of carbon and fluorine. When it was invented in 1938, it was the slipperiest substance known.

19

Noble Gases

The last column in the periodic table is group 18. The elements in this group are the noble gases, so-called because they stand apart from other elements. The atoms of these gases won't join with other atoms to make compounds. The noble gases are helium, neon, argon, krypton, xenon, and radon. They have no color or smell and are safe to use, apart from radioactive radon.

Inert Gases

The noble gases don't react because they have a full outer shell of electrons. This means that they have a valency, or bonding ability, of 0. They can't make bonds because they don't need to share, borrow, or lend electrons with other atoms. They exist as single atoms and, except for argon, are rare in nature. This element, however, makes up one percent of the air. We take argon in with every breath, but it has no effect on our bodies.

Argon is used as a shielding gas in welding.

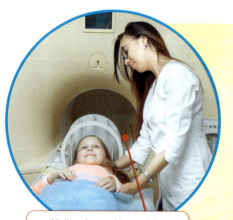

Helium is used to cool the magnets of MRI scanners. These are hospital machines used for looking inside our bodies.

Helium and Neon

The most familiar noble gases are helium and neon. Helium is lighter than air and so is used in balloons, but it's also an important cooling agent in spacecraft and advanced research equipment, such as the Large Hadron Collider. Neon is used as a powerful coolant in electrical equipment. It gives off a red glow when an electric current runs through it, so it's also commonly used in making bright lighted signs. The barcode scanners in stores use helium-neon gas lasers.

20 **DID YOU KNOW?** Nuclear reactors give off krypton. During the Cold War, measuring amounts of atmospheric krypton-85 helped track the secret building of nuclear weapons.

Red neon lights contain pure neon. Other colors are produced by the other noble gases. Neon lights are tubes containing the gases at low pressure with electricity running through them.

When electrons in neon signs are excited by electricity, they release energy as light. The different noble gases emit light of different wavelengths, which is why we see them as different colors.

The gases produce bright colors when an electric current gives energy to the electrons in their atoms.

Old-fashioned incandescent light bulbs emit light from a heated tungsten filament. The bulbs are full of argon, which keeps the heated filament from reacting with oxygen in the air.

HALL OF FAME

Marie Curie
1867–1934

Polish scientist Marie Curie and her husband, Pierre, discovered the elements radium and polonium from the mineral pitchblende. In 1900, they observed that radium released a gas during radioactive decay. The Curies were awarded a Nobel Prize in 1903, and Marie received a second one in 1911.

Metals

Metals are very dense elements, which can make them very strong. Yet, they are also malleable, meaning they can be molded into different shapes. They conduct heat and electricity well and have high melting and boiling points. These elements usually react with oxygen to form oxides and react with acids to make a metal salt compound plus hydrogen. Metals lose electrons in reactions to form positive ions called cations.

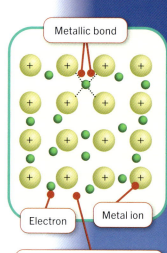

Metals are good conductors of electricity because of their metallic bonds. The outer electrons are loosely bonded and can flow between the atoms, carrying the charge through the metal.

Transition and Post-transition Metals

The transition metals, which fill the center of the periodic table, are typical metals. They are hard, heavy, shiny, and less reactive than the highly active alkali metals and alkaline earth metals. Iron, a transition metal, is attracted to magnets. Iron alloys are called ferrous metals and are also magnetic. The post-transition metals include aluminum and lead. They are softer than the transition metals and have lower melting points.

Electrolysis separates metal compounds that are dissolved or molten. Here, the electric current separates copper (Cu) from copper sulfate ($CuSO_4$) solution.

Separating Metals

Metals occur naturally in rocks as ores. They can be separated through methods such as electrolysis. Some metals, including zinc, iron, and copper, can be extracted using carbon. Carbon is a nonmetal that is more reactive than those metals, so it can remove them from their oxides and take their place, leaving pure metal behind.

HALL OF FAME

Jabir Ibn Hayyan
721–815

Jabir Ibn Hayyan was an alchemist born in Iran. He is known as the father of Arabic chemistry. He developed orderly ways to experiment and analyze substances, and he influenced theories of chemistry and modern pharmacy. Jabir is thought to have written hundreds of works describing chemical methods that included making alloys as well as purifying and testing metals.

Industrial sorting claws use magnets to separate ferrous metals, such as steel, from nonmagnetic materials, such as aluminum and plastics.

Because metals are so strong and malleable, they can be easily recycled. But first the waste must be sorted and separated.

Stainless steel is made from iron by adding chromium, which protects it from corrosion and rusting.

Alloys are often more useful than pure metals. Steel is an alloy of iron with carbon and other elements. It's stronger and lighter than iron, so it is used in cars and buildings.

DID YOU KNOW? The metal bismuth repels magnets. So, a magnet placed between two blocks of bismuth will float in the air between them!

Nonmetals and Semimetals

There aren't many nonmetal elements, but the ones that exist are vital to life. These include carbon that builds living cells and the oxygen that we breathe. Along the border of the metals and nonmetals are the semimetals, or metalloids.

Semiconductors

Semimetals are materials that conduct electricity under certain conditions. They are used to make semiconductors, which are used in many modern electronic devices. The semimetal silicon is like a metal because it's shiny and has a high melting point. But it's also like a nonmetal because it has a low density and is brittle. A pure silicon crystal can't conduct electricity because its electrons are tightly bonded. However, when atoms of an impurity, such as arsenic, are added to it, an electric current can flow. This allows electronic devices to be built around silicon.

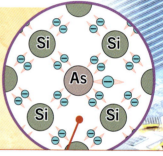

Adding arsenic to silicon adds extra free electrons, which carry a negative charge. Adding indium makes spaces without electrons. The spaces move as electrons flow into them, so they carry a positive charge.

Nonmetals

The nonmetal elements include hydrogen, carbon, nitrogen, oxygen, phosphorus, sulfur, and the halogens. The nonmetals look and behave in many different ways, but they are all unlike metals. They don't conduct heat or electricity well, and they have low melting and boiling points, as well as low densities. As solids, they break easily and are often brittle, so they are not easily shaped. Many are dull rather than shiny, and they are hardly magnetic at all.

The Kawah Ijen volcano in Indonesia emits sulfur that burns with a spectacular blue flame. Like other nonmetals, sulfur reacts with oxygen to produce acidic oxides, in this case, the blue-burning sulfur dioxide.

HALL OF FAME

Esther M. Conwell
1922–2014

Esther M. Conwell was an American chemist and physicist whose love of puzzles helped her explain how semiconductors work. She described how electrons flow through semiconductors in the Conwell-Weisskopf theory. This breakthrough revolutionized computing, boosting the development of everyday electronic devices. She received the Edison Medal in 1997 and the National Medal of Science in 2009.

Thousands of transistors fit on a silicone chip that is as small as a baby's fingernail. Tiny wires connect the components.

Silicon chips are inside all our electronic devices, from phones to solar panels.

Microprocessors are tiny processing units etched onto individual chips. They follow instructions and make decisions so the computer can do its work.

Silicon is used to make electronic on/off switches called transistors, which are used in computers.

DID YOU KNOW? In 1965, Gordon Moore correctly guessed that the number of transistors fitting on a silicon chip would double every year.

Molecules

Atoms like to stick together! Only a few—those that make up the noble gases—keep to themselves. Most atoms bond with other atoms to make molecules. Molecules can be composed of only a couple of atoms, or they can be giant molecular structures. A crystal is a structure in which the atoms or molecules join up in a regular, repeating pattern.

Diamond is the hardest natural substance on Earth. Many of these crystals are made into jewelry, but diamonds are also used in industrial tools.

Hydrogen is a diatomic element. By pairing up and sharing their electrons to make a bond, two hydrogen atoms make a stable, homonuclear molecule.

Diatomic Molecules

There are two atoms in diatomic molecules. If the atoms are identical, the molecule is homonuclear. Elements with atoms that pair up in this way are diatomic elements. The bond is made by sharing electrons, which fill up both atoms' energy shells. A hydrogen atom has one electron, but its shell can hold two—so two hydrogen atoms share their two electrons.

Allotropes

The crystals of some elements are simple. They contain only one kind of atom. Yet they can be surprising. Their atoms join together in different ways to make different allotropes. Two allotropes of carbon are diamond and graphite. Diamond and graphite have different properties because of the ways their atoms are arranged.

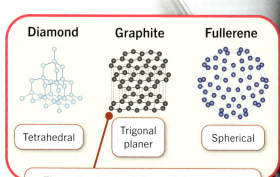

The molecular sheets in graphite are weakly bonded, so graphite is softer than diamond, which has strong bonds in all directions. Another allotrope—fullerene—has atoms in a sphere.

DID YOU KNOW? The largest uncut diamond ever found weighed more than 1 pound (0.45 kg). It was cut into more than 100 gemstones.

A pencil drawing is made of graphite. Both graphite and diamond are giant molecular structures of carbon.

Soft graphite is used in pencils because its molecules easily slide over one another and rub off on the paper, leaving a mark behind.

Crystals of the element sulfur can be shaped as four-sided pyramids or as long needles. These different forms are allotropes.

Rosalind Franklin
1920–1958
British scientist Rosalind Franklin studied molecules using X-ray crystallography. She helped to discover the double helix structure of the biological molecule deoxyribonucleic acid (DNA). She also made important discoveries about the structure of viruses, as well as about the different forms of carbon in coal and graphite. Her work on carbon paved the way for the development of useful carbon fiber technologies.

HALL OF FAME

Compounds

Compounds are molecules with more than one kind of atom. They are made when the atoms of different elements react and bond together. The different chemicals in a compound can be separated only by a chemical change that breaks their bonds.

Compound Properties

No atoms are lost when chemicals react. This means the total chemicals at the start and end of a reaction—the reactants and the products—contain the same atoms in different combinations. The products have new properties, meaning they look and behave differently from the reactants. When you drink water, you are drinking a liquid compound of the gases hydrogen and oxygen. When you lick salt, you are eating a compound of the gas chlorine and the metal sodium.

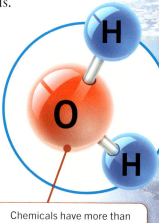

Chemicals have more than one name. A water molecule has two hydrogen atoms and one oxygen atom, so it is also called dihydrogen oxide.

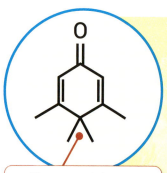

The structural chemical formula of 3,4,4,5-tetramethyl-2,5-cyclohexadien-1-one looks a bit like a penguin. Its common name is penguinone.

Names and Formulas

Some compounds contain many elements and have complicated names to describe them. Luckily, scientists give chemicals simpler common names as well. They also have a clever, short way of describing compounds through chemical formulas. Every element has a symbol of one or two letters, and these make up the chemical formulas of all possible compounds. The formula for water is H_2O, showing that the molecule has two hydrogen atoms and one oxygen atom. Chemists also use diagrams called structural chemical formulas to show the links between atoms.

DID YOU KNOW? Made in 2014, the largest molecule, PG5, contains 17 million atoms of carbon, nitrogen, and oxygen.

The terraces of Pamukkale in Turkey are a natural wonder formed by underground thermal springs rising to Earth's surface.

The beautiful white limestone pools are made out of calcium carbonate ($CaCO_3$), a compound of calcium, carbon, and oxygen that is carried up in water from underground.

Calcium carbonate is dissolved in liquid water underground. When the water cools at the surface, the $CaCO_3$ turns back into a solid.

The process of a dissolved chemical leaving the solution and becoming solid is called precipitation.

Marie-Anne Lavoisier
1758—1836

Marie-Anne Lavoisier and her husband Antoine had a laboratory at their home in Paris, where they invited other scientists to watch and debate their experiments. As Antoine's coworker, illustrator, translator, and assistant, Marie-Anne Lavoisier was essential to their shared research. Among other things, the couple identified oxygen and showed that it reacts with other elements to make compounds.

HALL OF FAME

Organic and Inorganic Chemicals

Atoms of carbon and hydrogen have a very important partnership. Compounds that contain carbon-hydrogen bonds are called organic compounds. All other compounds are inorganic. Organic chemistry is all about chains of atoms built off a backbone of carbon. This makes a series of chemicals with predictable structures and properties. The bodies of living things are made of organic chemicals that also contain other atoms, such as oxygen and nitrogen.

Hydrocarbons

Compounds that contain only carbon and hydrogen atoms are called hydrocarbons. A carbon atom can make four bonds, and a hydrogen atom can make one bond. So, the simplest hydrocarbon is one carbon atom linked by single bonds to four hydrogen atoms. This is the molecule methane (CH_4). Methane contains no double bonds, which makes it an alkaline that is a good fuel. It burns in oxygen to produce carbon dioxide, water, and energy.

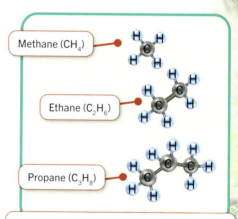

Methane (CH_4)
Ethane (C_2H_6)
Propane (C_3H_8)

Methane, ethane, and propane are the first three molecules in the alkane series. Each has one carbon and two hydrogen atoms more than the last, building up to very long chains.

HALL OF FAME

Saint Elmo Brady
1884–1966

Saint Elmo Brady was the first Black American chemist to be awarded a PhD in America. He studied carboxylic acids, or molecules with special arrangements of carbon, hydrogen, and oxygen. Brady examined how changing parts of a molecule affected its acidity. He improved ways of preparing and purifying organic acids. Brady also helped develop academic facilities at historically Black colleges and universities.

Polymerization

Monomers

A polymer molecule is a repeating structure, with molecules of the monomer linked up like beads on a chain.

Polymer

Monomers and Polymers

Polymers are long, repeating chains of many small molecules called monomers. Most, but not all, polymers are organic, and some occur naturally while others are synthetic. Plastics are synthetic polymers. The strong plastic polyvinyl chloride (PVC) is a long chain of linked vinyl chloride monomers containing carbon, hydrogen, and chlorine atoms. Natural polymers include fats, starches, proteins, and wool. Nucleic acids are natural polymers that carry the genetic information of living things.

Plastics are organic polymers made out of chemicals from fossil fuels. Plastic bottles are made from polymers such as polyethylene terephthalate, which is light, bendy, and easy to shape.

Glass bottles are made from an inorganic material, silicon dioxide (SiO_2) which is transparent, stiff, and brittle.

DID YOU KNOW? An average cow releases 82 gal. (310 L) of methane a day through burping and flatulence.

31

Covalent Bonds

Each energy shell of an atom can hold a certain number of electrons and must be full before another shell can be added. When atoms react and join up to make a molecule, a bond is made by the electrons in their outermost shells. How many bonds an atom can make is called its valency.

The Shared Bond

Atoms are most stable when their shells are full, so atoms will naturally attract electrons to fill up their energy shells. They can do this by sharing their electrons, making a covalent bond. The first shell of an atom holds up to two electrons. This explains why the two smallest atoms, hydrogen and helium, behave differently. A hydrogen atom, which has one electron, readily shares it with another atom. But a helium atom has two electrons, so it doesn't react because it is already stable.

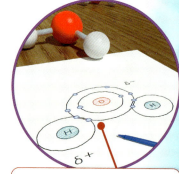

In a water molecule, the electrons donated by the oxygen atom fill up both hydrogen atoms' single shells. The electrons donated by the hydrogen atoms fill up the oxygen atom's second shell.

Double Bonds

A pair of electrons shared between two atoms makes a single covalent bond. Some atoms can also make a double bond by sharing two pairs of electrons. They can do this because the second and third shells can each hold up to eight electrons. An oxygen atom has six electrons in its second shell, so it has a valency of two. Two oxygen atoms can each donate two electrons to share between them, making eight electrons for each of their outer shells.

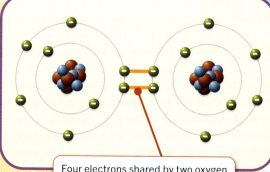

Four electrons shared by two oxygen atoms create a double bond in an oxygen molecule. The nuclei, with eight protons and eight neutrons each, remain unchanged.

DID YOU KNOW? In quantum physics, it seems an electron can spin in two directions at once and can affect another electron even across the galaxy.

HALL OF FAME

Linus Carl Pauling
1901–1994

Linus Carl Pauling was one of the first scientists to use quantum physics to describe how atoms make bonds in molecules. He was awarded the Nobel Prize in Chemistry for this work in 1954. He went on to be awarded the Nobel Peace Prize in 1962 for his efforts to ban nuclear weapons tests and end the threat of nuclear war.

Candles are made of paraffin wax, which becomes a fuel when the candle is lit.

The candle burns, producing heat and light, until all the wax is used up. This reaction is called combustion.

The hydrogen and carbon atoms in the candle wax make new covalent bonds with oxygen, producing carbon dioxide gas and water vapor.

Wax is a hydrocarbon. It has hydrogen and carbon atoms. When the candle burns, the heat melts the wax, which then turns into a vapor. Its molecular bonds are broken.

Ionic Bonds

Atoms stick together when an electrical force made by the electrons in their outermost energy shells makes a bond between them. In covalent bonds, the electrons are shared, but in ionic bonds the electrons move from atom to atom.

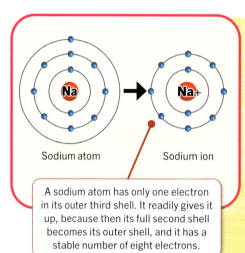

Sodium atom → Sodium ion

A sodium atom has only one electron in its outer third shell. It readily gives it up, because then its full second shell becomes its outer shell, and it has a stable number of eight electrons.

Ions

An atom usually has no charge. The negative charge of its electrons balances out the positive charge of its nucleus. When an atom loses or gains an electron, however, it loses or gains some charge and becomes a charged particle called an ion. If an electron moves away from an atom, it leaves an ion with a positive charge called a cation. An atom that gets an extra electron becomes a negative ion called an anion.

Ionic Lattices

The opposite charges of cations and anions attract each other by electrostatic force. This makes an ionic bond. Compounds containing ionic bonds are crystals with regular, repeating patterns of negative and positive ions in a lattice structure. The electrostatic force acts in all directions, making ionic lattices very strong. These compounds have no overall charge. The negative and positive charges balance each other out. They usually have high melting and boiling points, because a lot of energy is needed to break all the ionic bonds.

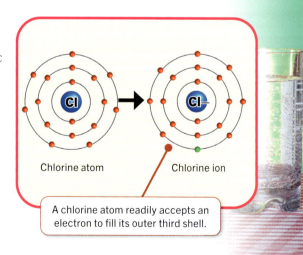

Chlorine atom → Chlorine ion

A chlorine atom readily accepts an electron to fill its outer third shell.

DID YOU KNOW? Our nerve cells use sodium and other ions to send electrochemical messages that travel at up to 180 miles per hour (290 kph).

Reactions

When substances react, the resulting products have new properties. The atoms of the reactants rearrange as their bonds break and new bonds form. No atoms are lost, so the same atoms are combined, albeit differently, in the reactants as were present in the products.

Chemical Equations

Chemists use equations to describe what happens in a reaction. A chemical equation uses chemical symbols and formulas to show the type and number of atoms in the molecules of the reactants and products. For example, the equation for the reaction of carbon and oxygen to make carbon dioxide is $C + O_2 \longrightarrow CO_2$. This equation shows that one atom of carbon reacts with two atoms of oxygen to make a carbon dioxide molecule containing one carbon and two oxygen atoms. The equation is balanced, with three atoms before the arrow and three atoms after it.

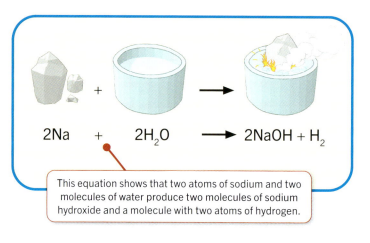

$2Na + 2H_2O \longrightarrow 2NaOH + H_2$

This equation shows that two atoms of sodium and two molecules of water produce two molecules of sodium hydroxide and a molecule with two atoms of hydrogen.

HALL OF FAME

Antoine Lavoisier
1743–1794

Antoine Lavoisier developed a theory of chemical reactivity that showed that the same amount of matter exists after a reaction as before. In 1789, he published a book stating this theory for the first time. The book also introduced a new way of naming compounds that is still the basis of chemical names today.

Reactivity

Reactivity is how readily a chemical reacts with others. Some metals, such as sodium, are so reactive that they can be found in nature only as compounds. Others, such as gold, are not reactive at all. Sodium is more reactive than copper, which is more reactive than silver, which is more reactive than gold. A more reactive metal will replace a less reactive metal in a compound in solution. This is called displacement.

When copper wire is suspended in a clear silver nitrate solution, copper atoms take the place of silver and change the solution to blue copper nitrate. The displaced silver forms crystals on the wire.

Atoms bond like a group of dancers holding hands. They can bond together, and then they can let go, move around, and find new partners.

The members of the group stay the same, even when they move around or change partners.

DID YOU KNOW? Chemical reactions keep us alive. Trillions of biochemical reactions are happening in your body right now.

Radioactivity

Each element has its own number of protons in its nucleus. But the number of neutrons is different in different isotopes. An isotope with more neutrons than usual is unstable and decays, giving off energy as radioactive particles and rays until it transforms into a more stable isotope or even a different element. This is a reaction called radioactivity.

Radioactivity disturbs the electrons of a gas in an instrument called a Geiger counter, helping people know when there is dangerous radiation nearby.

Half-life

When unstable isotopes—sometimes called radioisotopes—decay, their nuclei give off three types of radiation. The first is an alpha particle made of two protons and two neutrons. The second is beta radiation, which is when an atom sends out an electron. The third, gamma radiation, is a form of electromagnetic energy that moves in waves. This reaction changes the number of subatomic particles, which means that radioactive elements change into other elements. This radioactive decay occurs atom by atom, and it happens at different rates for different radioisotopes. A radioactive isotope's half-life is the time it takes for half of its nucleus to decay into the atoms of another element.

The age of pigments in prehistoric cave paintings can be found using carbon dating. Carbon-14 can date objects up to 60,000 years old.

Carbon Dating

Free neutrons that are not held in an atomic nucleus occur high in the atmosphere. When one bumps into a nitrogen atom in the air, the nitrogen gains a neutron and releases a proton. This changes the nitrogen into an atom of carbon-14. Carbon-14 atoms become part of carbon dioxide molecules and enter the food chain through plants. Carbon-14 is weakly radioactive. All living things contain a known percentage of it. When they die, those carbon-14 atoms decay slowly back into nitrogen. The half-life is 5,700 years. Scientists measure the amount of carbon-14 in organic matter to determine how old it is. This is called carbon dating.

DID YOU KNOW? Earth's background radiation causes changes to the genes inside of cells. These changes drive natural evolution.

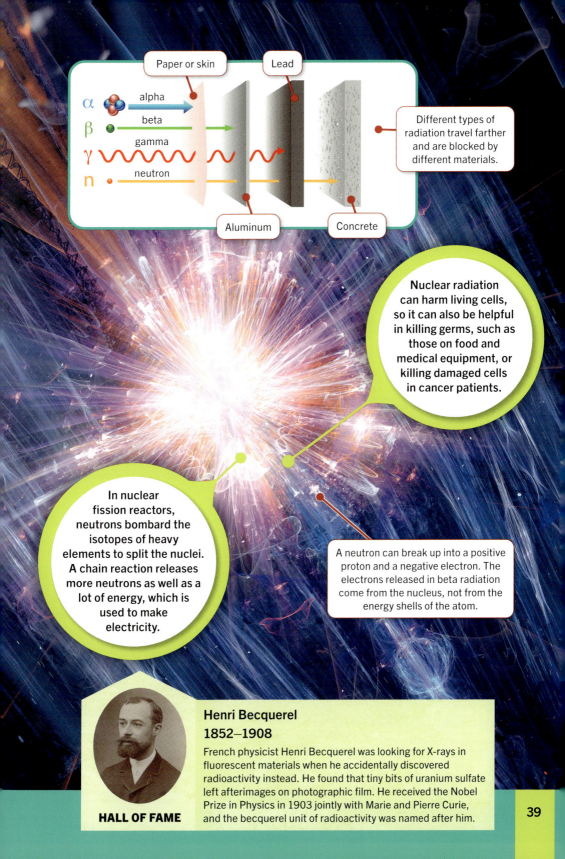

Different types of radiation travel farther and are blocked by different materials.

Nuclear radiation can harm living cells, so it can also be helpful in killing germs, such as those on food and medical equipment, or killing damaged cells in cancer patients.

In nuclear fission reactors, neutrons bombard the isotopes of heavy elements to split the nuclei. A chain reaction releases more neutrons as well as a lot of energy, which is used to make electricity.

A neutron can break up into a positive proton and a negative electron. The electrons released in beta radiation come from the nucleus, not from the energy shells of the atom.

Henri Becquerel
1852–1908

French physicist Henri Becquerel was looking for X-rays in fluorescent materials when he accidentally discovered radioactivity instead. He found that tiny bits of uranium sulfate left afterimages on photographic film. He received the Nobel Prize in Physics in 1903 jointly with Marie and Pierre Curie, and the becquerel unit of radioactivity was named after him.

HALL OF FAME

Important Properties

Every element and compound has unique properties because of its structure. We build with materials that have properties that make them fit for certain jobs. Hardness, roughness, flexibility, and permeability—or how much water can move through a material—are some of the most important physical properties of the materials humans use.

Metals and Ceramics

Metals are good for building because they're strong and malleable. They are also ductile, meaning they can be pulled into thin wires, and they conduct electricity and heat. Because of these properties, metals are used to move energy within electronic devices and through energy grids. Ceramics, such as porcelain and clay, are strong and waterproof, but they are also brittle. Ceramics are often used for mugs, toilets, bricks, and car brakes.

Ceramic tiles on the floor are smooth to walk on, long-lasting, and easy to clean.

Plastics and Rubber

Plastics are polymers made from fossil fuels. Plastics may be hard or soft, flexible or stiff, transparent or opaque. They come in many forms and are so versatile that we rely on plastics in nearly every industry.

A rubber band stretches because its molecules are long and tangled. When we pull it, the molecules straighten up and get longer. This stretching is reversible because the molecules eventually return to their old structure.

This boat is made of fiberglass, a material made of a combination of plastic and glass fibers. Fiberglass is strong like glass but also light like plastic.

40

HALL OF FAME

Angie Turner King
1905–2004

Angie Turner King's father encouraged her education, and she eventually earned a master's degree in mathematics and chemistry at Cornell University. King had a long career in science education. She taught chemistry to students as well as soldiers during World War II (1939–1945). Many of her students had outstanding careers in science.

Glass or transparent plastic lets sunlight into a greenhouse.

An apron made of waterproof cloth can keep a gardener's clothes dry. A material that doesn't allow water to soak through it is impermeable.

A plastic hose can bend around corners because it's flexible and stretchy.

Plant pots are often made of a stiff, opaque plastic. This holds the dirt in place and keeps too much water from leaking out, allowing the plants to get the water they need.

DID YOU KNOW? Diamond is the hardest natural substance on Earth. Diamond-edged tools are even used to drill rocks.

Elements and Compounds in Our Lives

From the DNA that forms our genes to the semiconductors that make our electronic devices work, our lives would not be possible without elements and compounds. In recent decades, both natural and synthetic compounds have been key to making innovative products, such as lightweight mobile devices and longer-lasting batteries for electric vehicles.

Difficult Reactions

Many medicines are created using complicated, ring-shaped molecules. These molecules are very difficult to work with because they often react to materials around them as soon as they are created. However, scientists have recently been able to remove other reactive elements from the air in their labs. This could make creating new medicines much easier.

Creating New Elements

Francium, discovered in 1939, was the last natural element to be discovered. Since then, scientists have discovered 28 synthetic elements. Although synthetic elements are difficult to make because they tend to break down immediately, the challenge isn't stopping scientists! Many think a new element could be created soon.

Scientists use particle accelerators to slam neutrons into atoms, creating new elements.

Superconducting Elements

Many scientists are working on ways to make the electric grid more efficient. Chemists are studying aluminum and mercury compounds that conduct electricity without much loss of energy when kept at very low temperatures. These superconductors could also create faster processors for computers.

43

Review and Reflect

Now that you've read about elements and compounds, let's review what you've learned. Use the following questions to reflect on your newfound knowledge and integrate it with what you already knew.

Check for Understanding

1. What determines the properties of an atom? *(p. 6)*

2. Name two ways an element can be identified. *(p. 8)*

3. On the periodic table, what do all elements in a period have in common? What do the elements in a group have in common? *(pp. 10-11)*

4. Why are alkali metals so reactive? *(p. 12)*

5. Name three compounds or objects that include an alkaline earth metal. *(pp. 16-17)*

6. What is sublimation? *(p. 18)*

7. Why are the elements in group 18 called the noble gases? *(p. 20)*

8. Explain why metals are good conductors of electricity. *(p. 22)*

9. In what ways are nonmetals different from metals? *(p. 24)*

10. What are two ways scientists label compounds? *(p. 28)*

11. What determines an atom's valency? *(p. 32)*

12. How does an ion form? What is the difference between an anion and a cation? *(p. 34)*

13. What does a chemical equation tell a chemist? *(p. 36)*

14. Describe what an isotope is. What happens when an unstable isotope decays? *(p. 38)*

15. List a different property for each of the following materials: metal, ceramic, plastic, and rubber. *(pp. 40-41)*

44

Making Connections

1. Choose one element from each of the major element groups described in this book. Use the periodic table to list the element's symbol and atomic number. Then, describe one way the element is used by people.

2. Choose two of the following element groups to compare and contrast: alkaline earth metals, halogens, noble gases, metals, or nonmetals and semimetals.

3. Explain the difference between a covalent bond and an ionic bond. What is an example of each?

4. Explain how a chemical formula shows what elements are present and how many of them form a compound. Find an example of a chemical formula in this book, and list which elements are included in it.

5. List the three types of radiation that radioisotopes give off when they decay. How can these types of radiation be beneficial?

In Your Own Words

1. Think of an object that you use every day. List some of the important properties it has that make it so useful to you.

2. Look at the following chemical formula: $C_{12}H_{22}O_{11}$. Using the periodic table, break down the elements and how many atoms of each are used to create this molecule. Then, research this chemical formula. What is the common name for this molecule, and how is it used?

3. Imagine you could sit down with one of the people from the Hall of Fame sidebars. What three questions would you like to ask them about their accomplishments?

4. In your opinion, which of the major element groups described in this book is the most useful in your day-to-day life? Why?

5. If you discovered a new element, what would you name it? What properties would it be possible for this new element to have?

45

Glossary

alloy a mixture of a metal with a different element

atom the smallest unit of a chemical element

atomic number the number of protons in an atom

chemical bond a force that holds atoms together

chemical reaction a process in which atoms are rearranged or undergo a chemical change

compound a chemical made from the atoms of more than one element

conductor a material that lets heat or electricity pass through it

crystal a solid material with particles joined together in a repeating lattice pattern

density the space a substance takes up in relation to the amount of matter in the substance

DNA deoxyribonucleic acid, a long molecule found in the cells that carries instructions for the structure and function of living things

electron a negatively charged particle found in an atom

element a chemical made of a single type of atom

formula the way scientists write down symbols to show the number and type of atoms present in a molecule

ion an atom that carries an electric charge because it has lost or gained an electron

isotopes forms of an element with different numbers of neutrons

molecule a group of two or more atoms that are chemically bonded

neutron a particle with no charge found in the nucleus of an atom

nucleus the center of an atom

organic chemicals carbon-based compounds used by living things

periodic table the system used to organize chemical elements by their atomic numbers

polymer a very large, chain-like molecule made of repeated smaller molecules

proton a positively charged particle found in the nucleus of an atom

radioactive giving off energy in the forms of small particles or waves

semiconductor a material that lets electricity pass through it under certain conditions

soluble the ability to dissolve in liquids, such as water

subatomic particles the particles that make up an atom

Read More

Dingle, Adrian. *My Book of the Elements (My Book).* New York: DK Publishing, 2024.

Farndon, John. *Periodic Table (Animated Science).* New York: Scholastic Press, 2021.

Jackson, Tom. *Matter & Energy (The World of Physics).* Minneapolis: Bearport Publishing Company, 2025.

McKenzie, Precious. *The Micro World of Atoms and Molecules (Micro Science).* North Mankato, MN: Capstone Press, 2022.

Learn More Online

1. Go to **FactSurfer.com** or scan the QR code below.
2. Enter "**Elements Compounds**" into the search box.
3. Click on the cover of this book to see a list of websites.

47

Index

acids 17, 22, 30–31
alkalis 10, 12, 16–17, 22, 30
atomic numbers 6, 8, 11–12
big bang 4
carbon dating 38
chemical reactions 37
combustion 33
covalent bonds 33–34
crystals 26, 34, 37
diamonds 26
DNA 27, 42
electricity 7, 9, 15, 21–22, 24, 35, 39, 40, 43
energy 6–7, 10–12, 14–16, 18, 21, 26, 30, 32, 34, 38–40, 43
energy shells 6, 10–12, 18, 26, 32, 34, 39
experiments 7, 29
fertilizers 12
fireworks 12, 16
food 19, 35, 38–39
fossil fuels 40
glass 40
gold 4, 8–9, 16, 37
graphite 26–27
halogens 10, 18–19, 24
inorganic chemicals 30
ionic bonds 34–35

magnets 20, 22–23
metals 8, 10–14, 16–17, 19, 22–24, 37, 40
monomers 31
nonmetals 10, 13, 24
organic chemicals 14, 30
periodic table 6, 10–12, 16, 18, 20, 22, 24
plants 38, 41
plastics 18, 23, 40
polymers 31, 40
radioactivity 38–39
reactions 22, 37
salt 13, 22, 28, 35
solutions 17
temperature 8, 16
X-rays 16, 27, 39